With You Wherever You Go

Written by Martine Foreman
Illustrated by QBN Studios

Copyright © 2021 by Martine Foreman

All rights reserved. No part of this book may be reproduced or used in any manner without the prior written permission of the copyright owner, except for the use of brief quotations in a book review.

ISBN 978-1-7368509-0-9

Library of Congress Control Number: 2021914503

Edited by Candice L. Davis
Illustrations by Quynh Nguyen of QBN Studios

One Nine Press
Columbia, Maryland

martineforeman.com

To mommy—thank you for believing in me and always
teaching me that God is with me wherever I go.

To Uncle Roro—thank you for choosing me.
I miss you dearly.

To Sean, Malachi, Jada, and Shiloh—
I carry your love with me wherever I go.

This book belongs to

_____

When it's rainy outside
and clouds cover the sky,
and you feel so down,
but you aren't quite sure why,
I want you to remember,
I need you to know,
God will be with you
wherever you go.

When the sun sets too early
and you don't want to play,
and you feel like it's been
a gloomy, glum day,
don't ever forget,
make sure that you know,
God will be with you
wherever you go.

When you eat a treat
or have fun with a friend,
and your day is so sweet
you hope it won't end,
hold on to those feelings
and don't let them go
because God will be with you
wherever you go.

When things change too fast
and you miss what once was,
and you find yourself scared
or sad just because,

When someone is mean
and just seems unkind,
and you wish you could leave
all those mean words behind,
have faith and be strong.
Let your smile help you glow,
and know that God's with you
wherever you go.

When you're met with surprises and enjoy each delight, when you're joyful all day and you rest well at night,

find peace in this truth, which you surely know. God is there with you wherever you go.

When life seems unfair
and you feel like you've lost,
and you want to go backwards
whatever the cost,

When things are confusing
and you can't find your way,
when you're not sure what to do
or what words to say,
the wonderful truth is,
whether you feel happy or low,
God will be with you
wherever you go.

When you get to smile
and laugh all day long,
and life feels like
one long, happy song,

just remember who's with you.
Be sure that you know.
Of course, God is with you
wherever you go.

When life feels hard
and things make you sad,
and you wonder what's next
or you even feel mad,
I hope you remember,
more than all things you know,
God will be with you
wherever you go.

When you are afraid
and hiding seems best,
when your courage within
is put to the test,
I pray you remember,
I pray that you know,
God is always there with you
wherever you go.

And when all things seem to go just your way, when you're happy, excited and grateful each day,

I want you to remember,
as you learn and you grow,
God always stays with you
wherever you go.

Made in the USA
Middletown, DE
04 November 2021